Girls'

BASKETBALL

by Doug Williams

GIRLS'
SportsZone

Published by ABDO Publishing Company, PO Box 398166, Minneapolis, MN 55439. Copyright
© 2014 by Abdo Consulting Group, Inc. International copyrights reserved in all countries. No part of
this book may be reproduced in any form without written permission from the publisher. SportsZone™
is a trademark and logo of ABDO Publishing Company.

Printed in the United States of America,
North Mankato, Minnesota

052013
092013

 THIS BOOK CONTAINS AT LEAST 10% RECYCLED MATERIALS.

Editor: Chrös McDougall
Series Designer: Marie Tupy

Photo Credits: Shutterstock Images, cover, 1, 44; Cal Sport Media via AP Images, 5, 8, 41; Stacy Bengs/
AP Images, 7; Genevieve Ross/AP Images, 10, 13; Stacy Bengs/AP Images, 15; Danny Moloshok/AP
Images, 18; Fred Beckham/AP Images, 21; Jessica Hill/AP Images, 23; Bob Child/AP Images, 25;
Darron Commungs/AP Images, 28; Charles Krupa/AP Images, 29, 31, 34; Jae C. Hong/AP Images,
32; Eric S. Lesser/AP Images, 42

Library of Congress Control Number: 2013902402

Cataloging-in-Publication Data

Williams, Doug.
 Girls' basketball / Doug Williams.
  p. cm. -- (Girls' sportszone)
 ISBN 978-1-61783-984-9 (lib. bdg.)
 Includes bibliographical references and index.
 1. Basketball for girls--Juvenile literature.   I. Title.
 796.323--dc23

                                                      2013902402

Table of Contents

1

Jump Shooting with Maya Moore

I t was early in the third quarter when Maya Moore started to put on a show. Her Minnesota Lynx were trailing the Indiana Fever 47–42. That's when Moore took a pass from teammate Lindsay Whalen just outside the three-point line to the right of the key.

Moore set her feet, squared her body to her target, and jumped. She launched her shot toward the basket. The orange and white ball spun through the air on its long arc and fell right through the middle of the hoop. *Swish.*

Just like that, the Lynx had cut the score to 47–45. Moore, however, was just getting warmed up.

Minnesota Lynx guard Maya Moore rises above a New York Liberty defender for a jump shot.

Moore's jump-shooting display on September 17, 2012, in Minneapolis lasted just over six-and-a-half minutes. It turned an ordinary midseason Women's National Basketball Association (WNBA) game into something special. Moore's performance would be remembered in the record books.

Whalen fed Moore another pass two minutes after the first three-pointer. Moore received it on the right baseline. She launched another three-point shot. It again hit nothing but net.

Next Moore took a pass from Candice Wiggins in the opposite corner. Moore put up another three-point shot. This time the ball hit the rim, rolled around, and fell through the basket. About a minute later, Moore took a pass from Monica Wright. She finished the play with a long three-pointer from the right side of the court.

Whalen drove to the basket on the Lynx's next trip down the

PICTURE-PERFECT SHOOTER

Katie Smith ranks as one of the all-time great scorers in women's basketball history. The 5-foot-11 guard played on three gold-medal-winning US Olympic teams. She also has two WNBA championships. Smith is known for having perhaps the most technically sound form on her jump shot. She was the first woman in US pro basketball to reach 5,000 points. Through 2012 she also shared the WNBA record for points in a game, with 47. Says Olympic teammate Tina Thompson: "When Katie Smith shoots the ball, her jumper is pure."

floor. But Whalen's shot was blocked. Whalen grabbed the ball and passed it out to Moore. She was alone beyond the three-point line in the left corner. Moore set her feet, locked her gaze on the basket, and jumped. She sent the ball on a high path that ended at the center of the hoop.

The third quarter soon came to an end. The Lynx had outscored the Fever 25–22. Fifteen of those points came from Moore's five three-pointers. Her five three-pointers in a quarter set a team record and tied a WNBA record. She finished the night with a career-best 29 points in Minnesota's 86–79 victory.

Maya Moore celebrates a Minnesota Lynx win over the Atlanta Dream in a 2012 WNBA game.

"Just one of those nights where the shot's feeling good, so you keep shooting," Moore said after the game. "And my teammates found me."

The outstanding shooting performance was just one of many in Moore's long career. She was only 23. Yet by then she had been an All-American at the University of Connecticut, an Olympic gold medalist for Team USA, and a WNBA champion.

Moore is a well-rounded player who can pass, rebound, and play defense. But she is best known as a scorer. Her accurate jump shot gives

Katie Douglas of the Indiana Fever shoots a three-point shot during a 2012 game.

her the ability to score against almost any defense and from beyond the three-point line.

The Jump Shot

Moore makes the jump shot look easy. She can rise above defenders and nail shots from all over the court. Making jump shots is no easy task, though. Many professional players make less than 50 percent of their jump shots in games. So any team that has good jump shooters has a great advantage.

There are other ways players can score in basketball. The layup is a common shot. Free throws are important too. It takes a lot of practice to become skilled at making those shots. Jump shots might be the hardest to make. That is especially true for long-range three-pointers. The best scorers often take hundreds of practice shots between games.

The first key to a good jump shot is finding a balanced position. The player's feet and body should be square to the basket. That means the body

SHE KNOWS HER SPOTS

Katie Douglas was known as one of the WNBA's best jump shooters. She showed why in the 2006 WNBA All-Star Game. Douglas scored 11 points in the first quarter of a 98–82 win over the West. She made three three-pointers in the first 10 minutes. Overall, she was 4-of-7 on three-pointers, scored 16 points, and was named the game's Most Valuable Player (MVP). Douglas was going to her favorite shooting spots, and her teammates were getting the ball to her. "They made things easy for me," said Douglas.

should be directly facing the hoop. Then the player must jump upward. The goal is to release the shot at the highest point of the jump. This makes it harder for a defender to block the shot.

Shooting fundamentals are also key. In a jump shot, the player's off hand steadies the ball. Then the shooting hand extends upward and launches the ball toward the hoop with a flick of the wrist. The shooting hand should always follow through toward the basket for maximum accuracy. The mechanics should be the same on every jump shot.

Maya Moore puts up a jump shot for the Minnesota Lynx during a 2012 game against the Tulsa Shock.

Quick Tip: Around the World

Even the best players have their sweet spots. These are places on the court where they are the most comfortable—and successful—shooting the ball. It is important to be versatile, though. Life is easier for a defender if you shoot from the same spot all game. One way to practice shooting from different locations is a game called Around the World. With a partner, pick six spots on the court. One player starts by shooting from the first spot. If she makes it, she moves on to the next spot. If she misses the shot, then the other player takes over. The first person to travel "around the world" by making a shot from all six spots wins.

A good jump shooter makes life harder for defenders. They always have to guard a good shooter closely. However, tight defense means the offensive player can then more easily dribble past the defender. In addition, good jump shooters can be more effective against zone defenses. In zones, teams pack their defenders closer to the basket to guard an area, rather than an individual. Of course the most important benefit of good jump shooting is that it allows a player to score from all over the court.

"The hardest people to guard are the ones who can get up off the ground, because it's hard to contest their shot," Moore said of good jump shooters. "[Players] who can get off the ground quickly and with some height. If you guard people who are consistent and on balance who just have a knack for shooting the ball, you just have to hope they miss."

2

Passing with Lindsay Whalen

Lindsay Whalen caught the basketball near the half-court line. She immediately scanned the court with her eyes. Whalen found her Minnesota Lynx teammate Maya Moore. Moore was sprinting uncovered toward the basket. In an instant, Whalen launched a two-handed pass. The basketball flew almost 50 feet (15.2 m) through the air and over several Tulsa Shock defenders.

The ball came down exactly where it was aimed. Moore caught it in full stride just a couple of feet from the hoop. Without even having to dribble, she made an easy layup.

Lindsay Whalen of the Minnesota Lynx takes the ball up the court during a 2012 WNBA game.

The basket gave the Lynx a 35–31 lead in the second quarter of the home game on July 12, 2012.

Whalen had also connected with Moore just 20 seconds before. That time Whalen saw Moore break free from her defender along the baseline. So Whalen made a quick pass that resulted in an easy bucket.

Basketball fans have gotten used to seeing Whalen make plays like that. She has an eye for finding holes in defenses and then making sharp passes. Her eight assists that night in Minneapolis helped the Lynx beat Tulsa 89–74. Her 5.4 assists per game led the WNBA that season. One year earlier she had a WNBA-leading 5.9 assists per game. The Lynx won the league championship that year.

In addition, Whalen was a key player for Team USA at the 2012 Olympic Games. Whalen shared point guard duties with

WHO'S NO. 1?

Sue Bird is one of the world's best point guards. She has won championships with her college team (University of Connecticut) and her WNBA team (Seattle Storm). Plus she also won three gold medals with Team USA in 2004, 2008, and 2012. As the point guard, she has been the leader on the floor for every team. After the 2012 WNBA season she ranked second in career assists. "I think Sue's been playing awesome her whole life," said her Storm teammate Lauren Jackson. "I think she's the best point guard in the world, no doubt about it."

fellow WNBA star Sue Bird. They helped the United States claim its fifth straight gold medal in women's basketball.

"She has tremendous body control, and when you dribble low like she does, nobody is going to steal it," Bird said. "She's deceptively quick and so low, you never know if she'll dish it or shoot it."

As a point guard, Whalen knows the success of the offense starts with her. It's her job to bring the ball up the court. So she must establish the tempo. The point guard also must break down defenses with passes. She wants to get the basketball to teammates who are in good position to score or to make good passes of their own. This requires point guards to always be aware of where their teammates are and what they are doing.

Lindsay Whalen, *right*, looks for a pass during a 2012 WNBA playoff game against the Los Angeles Sparks.

"You're just trying to see the next play as it's happening," Whalen said. "Reading where the [defensive] help is coming from. . . . Reading where your teammates are on the floor and if they're in good position. Getting rid of the ball as quickly as possible before the defense can rotate [to help]."

Seimone Augustus plays with Whalen on the Lynx and was also on the 2012 US Olympic team. Augustus said Whalen is an unselfish player who makes everybody on the floor better.

"She does an incredible job finding us and putting us in position to score baskets," Augustus said. It is no wonder Augustus likes playing with Whalen. Together they have won a WNBA title and an Olympic gold medal.

Passing All the Tests

Basketball teams need to score points in order to win games. Quick and effective passing is the best way to set up an offense. That is because the basketball can be moved much more quickly by passing than by dribbling.

An outlet pass can start a fast break down the court. Passes in a half-court set can get the ball to open players or expose gaps in a defense. Plus, passing allows a team to keep all of its players involved on offense. That makes it harder for defenders to focus on one player or one area of the court.

Whalen also has another way to be a passing threat. "The biggest thing I've been able to do throughout my career is really get to the basket and finish well," Whalen explained. "That usually draws the defense." She then can decide to shoot or to pass the ball to players left open by defenders who switched to her.

There are four main styles of passing. The most common is the two-hand chest pass. This is when a player passes the ball as if she is pushing it away from her body. Chest passes often send the ball through the air. However, sometimes a bounce pass works better. Having a pass bounce once off the floor can help it move through tight spaces between defenders.

Basketball players sometimes use an overhead pass. These passes are delivered by throwing the ball with two hands above the head. This pass is useful for throwing the ball over shorter opponents. It can also be used if a defender is marking the passer very tight. The fourth type of pass, the baseball pass, is a one-armed overhead pass. It looks just like

PORTUGUESE PASSING WIZ

Ticha Penicheiro might be the flashiest passer ever to play in the WNBA. She became known for her behind-the-back and no-look passes to teammates. Penicheiro was college basketball's Player of the Year at Old Dominion. Then she played 15 pro seasons and became the first player in the WNBA to reach 2,000 career assists. She retired in 2012 as the WNBA's all-time leader with 5.7 assists per game. She also led the league in assists seven times.

throwing a baseball. This is useful when a player needs to move the ball a long distance.

Excellent passers such as Whalen follow certain fundamentals on chest passes. They step toward the pass receiver with one foot. This helps send the ball with force and accuracy. Following through with the passing motion also helps accuracy. The goal is to get the ball safely to a teammate so she is in a position to score or make another good pass.

Lindsay Whalen sends a pass to a teammate during a 2012 game against the Connecticut Sun.

Quick Tip: Step Toward the Target

Like any good passer, Lindsay Whalen usually steps toward her target when making a pass. Passing is an easy skill to practice, even if you are alone. First find a sturdy wall outside and pick a target on the wall. Then stand a few feet away from the wall and practice passing toward that target. You can do chest passes or bounce passes. Just make sure you step toward the target each time. Once you get the hang of it, start stepping back after each successful pass. See if you can get back to 10 feet (3 m) away.

Passing is about more than technique, though. A good passer also needs to know how to read her teammates. She will know where her teammates are at all times. Then she will know where they are going. Players like Whalen often pass the ball not to a teammate but instead to a space where the teammate will soon be.

Whalen has great technique. She also reads the game exceptionally well. Those abilities helped her break the Lynx's career assist record in 2012.

"She just understands where people are going to be," Lynx coach Cheryl Reeve said.

chapter 3

Rebounding with Tina Charles

Renee Montgomery could see her path to the basket was open. So she quickly made a move toward the hoop. The Connecticut Sun guard dribbled once and then leaped high. She put up a soft, one-handed shot. But the basketball bounced off the glass, hit the rim, and then fell away to the left side of the basket.

There, waiting for its arrival, was teammate Tina Charles. Charles went up over an Indiana Fever defender to grab the ball with both hands. Immediately, she put up a shot that banked off the glass and through the hoop. Charles was fouled on her shot. She then made a free throw to complete a three-point play.

Tina Charles pulls down a rebound for the Connecticut Sun during a
2010 WNBA game against the Phoenix Mercury.

COLLEGE STAR

Courtney Paris has had an up-and-down WNBA career. But the 6-foot-4 center ranks as the best rebounder in women's college basketball history. Paris was a four-time All-American at the University of Oklahoma from 2006 to 2009. She still held the record for most rebounds in a career (2,034) and season (539 in 2006) through 2012. She was also still the only college player, male or female, with 2,000 rebounds and 2,500 points. She was such a consistent player that she set a national record with 112 straight "double-doubles." Those are games when a player gets at least 10 rebounds and 10 points.

Her rebound, basket, and free throw gave Connecticut a 50–43 lead in Game 1 of the 2012 WNBA Eastern Conference Finals. It ended a dominant third quarter for Charles.

She grabbed six rebounds and scored 10 points over the first nine minutes of the quarter. Three times in the quarter, Charles was able to get the rebound of a teammate's missed shot. Each time those rebounds led to Sun baskets. The Sun outscored the Fever 20–13 during that time.

Connecticut went on to win 76–64. "In the second half, I just wanted to set the tone, just getting on the [offensive] boards as much as I could to score," she said.

The rebounding effort was nothing unusual for Charles. She averaged 10.5 rebounds per game in 2012. That gave her a third consecutive WNBA rebounding title. Charles had pulled down 398 rebounds during her rookie season in 2010. That was good for 11.7 per game and the league's Rookie of the Year Award. She won a bigger honor in 2012: the league's MVP Award.

Charles is considered the finest rebounder in women's basketball. She might even be the best ever. She stands tall at 6 feet, 4 inches. But Charles

Tina Charles of the Connecticut Sun, *right*, and Tamika Catchings of the Indiana Fever, *left*, battle for position to get a rebound in 2012.

PLAYING THE ANGLES

When Lisa Leslie was in high school, she wanted to increase her leaping ability. So she joined the volleyball and track and field teams. Her hard work paid off. Leslie became one of the greatest college, Olympic, and WNBA players of all time. When she retired after the 2009 season, the 6-foot-5 star was the WNBA's all-time rebounding leader with 3,307. She led the league in three seasons.

Leslie said one of the ways to become a great rebounder is to become a student of the game.

"The first thing I think about is where the ball is shot from, because a lot of rebounds are just based on the angles," she once said. "A shot from the baseline will more than likely end up coming out to the other baseline. My goal is to get there or get around my opponent as much as possible."

has a rare combination of height, jumping ability, quickness, and technique. She has starred in the WNBA, for the US Olympic team, and at the University of Connecticut.

"It's mostly effort," former Connecticut Sun coach Mike Thibault said. "You have to have timing. . . . There are people with great rebounding skills, but not wills. She has the will to go get [the ball]."

Asjha Jones is a teammate on the Sun. She says Charles is quick for her size, but what really sets Charles apart is her smarts. Charles always seems to know where the ball is going to come off the rim.

"That's a skill that people kind of take for granted and don't talk about much," Jones said. "Being able to read the flight of the ball and know where it's going to come off is a skill people really don't have, and she has a natural knack for that. It's a talent."

Grabbing Boards

Even the best basketball players miss a lot of shots. That makes rebounding an important part of the game. For the defense, a rebound changes the possession without allowing the other team to score. For the offense, a rebound keeps a possession alive. Plus, offensive rebounds often lead to

Los Angeles Sparks center Lisa Leslie pulls in a rebound during a 2005 game.

easy second-chance shots right under the basket. The team that rebounds better is often the team that wins.

Every player on the court can and should try to grab rebounds. However, forwards and centers are usually called on to rebound more. That is because they are usually taller and set up closer to the basket. Charles often plays very close to the basket in her center position.

"I know that my team needs me to get rebounds," she said. "We know our jobs as post players is to go at the glass every time we can, every opportunity. Sometimes, even if I don't get the ball, [I will] make sure I'm boxing out my [opponent]."

The Connecticut Sun's Tina Charles blocks out during the 2012 WNBA playoffs.

Quick Tip: Keep Arms and Hands Up

When Tina Charles gets into rebounding position, she keeps her arms and hands up. That allows her to more easily control the ball when it comes to her. Boxing out is important to gain position. But it is harder to grab a rebound or maintain possession if you have to tip the ball away or try to catch it with one hand. One way to practice this is simply by getting in the habit of keeping your arms up on defense. Even in practice, never take a play off.

There are many techniques and qualities that make a good rebounder. Perhaps the most important is positioning. The foundation of many rebounds is "boxing out." This is when a player positions herself so that she is facing the basket and standing between the rim and the player she is guarding. The player who is boxing out then spreads her legs to get a sturdier base. By putting her arms up and flexing her knees, she can be ready to jump and get the ball when it comes off the rim or backboard.

Quickness is also key. Rebounders want to get off the floor quickly and go after the ball with both hands. Rebounding is more than technique and quickness, though. Rebounding is hard work. Good rebounders anticipate that every shot will be missed and hustle to get good position when every shot goes up.

chapter 4

Defense with Tamika Catchings

T he WNBA published a scouting report on all of the US players before the 2012 Olympic Games in London, England. One of the players was Tamika Catchings. The report on Catchings began with a statement about her style of play.

"The reigning WNBA Most Valuable Player is the best two-way player in the league, impacting every aspect of the game on a nightly basis," it read. "She is arguably the best defensive player that the WNBA has ever seen and the most intense player whenever she steps on the court."

The rest of the world was quickly reintroduced to Catchings's defensive talents and energy in London. Team USA opened with an 81–56 win over Croatia. Catchings had two steals in that game. She added three more

Team USA's Tamika Catchings, *top*, and France's Emmeline Ndongue battle for a rebound during the 2012 Olympic Games in London.

DOMINANT DOWN LOW

Chicago Sky center Sylvia Fowles is a talented scorer. But the 6-foot-6 Fowles might also be the WNBA's best interior defender and shot blocker. She was the 2011 WNBA Defensive Player of the Year after leading all players in blocked shots for the second straight year. Fowles also played on the 2012 US Olympic team. She makes her presence felt against every opponent. Seattle Storm guard Katie Smith said Fowles is "strong, she can jump, and she's just relentless. She's a handful."

steals as Team USA won its next four games. The United States played Canada in the quarterfinals. Catchings was all over the court again. She collected four steals and pulled down six rebounds in the 91–48 win.

"For our team, our defense leads to our offense," Catchings said after the win over Canada. "When we play really good defense, we get a lot of really good looks on the offensive end."

Team USA eventually met undefeated France in the gold-medal game. And once again Catchings was at the top of her game. She led a defense that forced 21 turnovers. Plus Catchings had two of her team's eight steals.

The key stretch for Team USA was in the second half. France had closed the United States' lead to 41–31. Then Team USA scored 13 of the next 14 points. After that the Americans cruised to an 86–50 victory. It was also their forty-first consecutive Olympic win and fifth straight gold medal. And at the center of that second-half run was a defensive play by Catchings.

Catchings stole the ball from a French dribbler. Then she quickly passed to teammate Sue Bird in the middle of the court. Bird threw a long pass to Maya Moore for an easy layup. It was as easy as 1–2–3. The Americans had another basket, courtesy of Catchings's defense.

The play is typical of the way Catchings has played throughout her standout career. The 6-foot-1 forward has been a respected scorer and rebounder at the University of Tennessee, in the WNBA, and on three Olympic gold-medal teams. But it is her defense that has made her special. In 2012, she was selected as the WNBA's Defensive Player of the Year for

Tamika Catchings, *left*, of Team USA reaches for a loose ball against the Czech Republic during the 2012 Olympic Games in London.

a record fifth time. She is the league's all-time leader in steals. And she has led the league in steals six times. Catchings also is among the league's career leaders in blocked shots and rebounds.

"She always impacts the game down the stretch with big-time defensive plays," said Gary Kloppenburg, who was an assistant coach with Catchings's WNBA team, the Indiana Fever. "[She gets] a rebound, a blocked shot, a steal. There's nobody you'd want besides her at the end of the game to be out there defensively."

Candace Parker, *left*, of the Los Angeles Sparks smothers San Antonio Silver Stars player Danielle Adams during a 2012 WNBA playoff game.

Defense Is Key

Catchings said she became a good defensive player when she played for coach Pat Summitt at Tennessee. Summitt stressed defense as something that can make a difference in every game.

"One thing I know is, my shot might not fall, but the biggest difference I can make every single day is my defensive intensity," Catchings said.

Many of the most successful teams stress defense as a way to win championships. A team's shooting may go cold. Or a team might have trouble rebounding against a taller team. But defensive effort is something a team can depend on every game. That has been the case since Catchings joined the Fever in 2002.

"We've heard from players who have joined our team . . . who got in here and said, 'We hated playing Indiana because of your defense,' " Fever General Manager Kelly Krauskopf said. "Obviously, Catch is the catalyst, the leader, in terms of that identity."

DEFENSE PRODUCES OFFENSE

Candace Parker is one of the WNBA's most exciting offensive players. Yet the 6-foot-4 All-Star and Olympic gold medalist takes great pride in her defense. In fact, she says playing strong defense leads to offensive opportunities. For example, a steal or block can lead to a fast break against a defense scrambling to get back. "When I play defense it gives me an advantage because I'm in the open court," she said. "So it's a win-win situation."

A team that plays strong defense can count on a number of benefits. Good defense can force the other team to take low-percentage shots. It can also force a team to make mistakes. Bad passes and turnovers can lead to easy baskets for the other team. Good defense can also take a team out of its offensive rhythm. That forces the offense to work extra hard for scoring opportunities, which can wear it out.

There are two main defensive systems. One is man-to-man. This is when every player guards an opponent. The other is zone. This is when players are responsible for guarding an area of the court. The goal is to try to limit an opponent's close, easy shots. Man-to-man defense is a more

Tamika Catchings of Team USA traps Canada's Teresa Gabriele during the 2012 Olympic Games in London.

Quick Tip: Defense Starts with Stance

Defense starts with a well-balanced stance. Your weight should be slightly forward on the balls of your feet and your knees flexed. Your head should be up for good vision. And your hands are ready to challenge a pass, a dribble, or a shot. While defending, your hand should be up high on the ball side of the ball handler (the better to move against a pass) and down low on the non-ball side (to be able to defend against a cross-over dribble). With your feet just a bit wider than your shoulders, you are able to quickly move from side to side.

active scheme that might force an opponent into more mistakes. However, the traits that produce good defensive players and a strong team defense are similar.

Defensive players must always hustle and be responsible for their player or area. They must challenge players with the ball. And they must be quick and use good footwork and anticipate passes and shots. With strong fundamentals and desire, a player such as Catchings can be a difference-maker every game.

"She can guard pretty much anybody on the court," Kloppenburg said. "She can guard anybody from 5-foot-2 to 6-foot-5 with her ability to defend. She's just so versatile and such a fierce rebounder. She is the backbone of a pressure defensive system."

chapter 5

Ball Handling with Sue Bird

The clock read 20.4 seconds. The scoreboard read 77–77. Most fans in Seattle's KeyArena were too nervous to sit for the end of Game 1 of the 2010 WNBA Finals. Seattle Storm point guard Sue Bird appeared to be the calmest person in the building.

Bird stood near half court, bent over at the waist with her head up, surveying the scene. She dribbled the basketball with her right hand. The Atlanta Dream's 6-foot-4 Sancho Lyttle stood guard a few feet away. But Bird paused.

The seconds ticked off the clock. With the clock down to nine seconds, Bird began to move. She dribbled to a spot just above the top of the key. Then she quickly darted to the right toward her teammate, Lauren Jackson.

Seattle Storm point guard Sue Bird dribbles the basketball during Game 3 of the 2010 WNBA Finals against the Atlanta Dream.

A "T-SPOON" OF LEARNING

Teresa Weatherspoon might have been the best point guard of her era. She starred on three levels, first at Louisiana Tech, then in the WNBA, and also on the US Olympic team.

The 5-foot-8 player nicknamed "T-Spoon" was an outstanding dribbler. She was also the league's all-time assist leader when she retired in 2004. She once said that she learned to dribble as a four-year-old in Texas, playing on "a bumpy patch of dirt and grass." Learning how to control the basketball on such an uneven surface turned her into one of the world's most skilled ball handlers.

As Bird moved to her right, Lyttle followed her. Lyttle rushed around Jackson. She got in position to deny Bird an open shot when Bird came around Jackson's screen.

Suddenly, however, Bird stopped. She planted her right foot and pushed off to her left. She flicked the ball on a bounce from her right hand to her left hand as her body moved to her left. It was a perfect cross-over dribble. Lyttle was now trapped behind Jackson. So Bird had created a wide-open shot 18 feet (5.5 m) from the basket.

Bird set her feet, squared her body toward the basket, and put up a high-arcing jump shot. It plunged through the net with 2.6 seconds on the clock. Bird's shot gave the Storm a 79–77 victory. Seattle would go on to sweep the series 3–0 to earn its second WNBA championship.

For Bird, it was another great play in a great career. She had been college basketball's Player of the Year at the University of Connecticut. Then she was the first overall pick in the WNBA Draft. Bird was later selected as one of the league's top 15 players ever. In addition, she has been a point guard on three US Olympic-champion teams.

"We were just going to let Sue be Sue," said Storm coach Brian Agler of Bird's game-winning play.

That put a lot on Bird's shoulders. The Dream had just scored five points to tie the game. Seattle called timeout with 20.4 seconds remaining and drew up a play to put the ball in Bird's hands. From the moment she took the inbounds pass, she was in control.

Bird said her plan was first to run down the clock. Then she would dribble toward Jackson and lose her defender to create an opening for a shot or pass.

"I had a feeling that if I went off the [screen] and brought it back to the same side that I'd just come from . . . I was going to be able to get a look," Bird said of her cross-over dribble move.

It was her shot that won the game. But it was Bird's ability to handle the basketball and move quickly while dribbling that set it up. The 5-foot-9 Bird is a terrific shooter and passer. But her skills as a ball handler give her

IT'S IN THE GLOVES

In 2011, Becky Hammon became just the seventh player in WNBA history to score 5,000 points. A big part of her scoring ability comes from her skills as a ball handler. In 2007, the 5-foot-6 guard won the league's skills contest called "Dribble, Dish, and Swish." She scores many baskets off drives that involve dribbling past defenders through the crowded lane. Hammon said one thing she's done through the years to sharpen her ball handling skills is to go through dribbling drills wearing thick gardening gloves.

the ability to drive to the basket, move through traffic, and dribble away from defenders.

"She's not just the best point guard in America right now," said Geno Auriemma, who coached her at Connecticut and with the US Olympic team. "Sue is the best point guard in the world right now. She's a tremendous ball handler and passer. She just sees the game; she understands it."

While at Connecticut, Bird three times won the Nancy Lieberman Award. It is given to the best point guard in college basketball based on "floor leadership, playmaking, and ball handling skills."

Bird was the most efficient ball handler in the league during the Storm's 2010 championship season. She rarely turned the ball over, yet she was second in the league in assists. For every turnover she made, she had 3.2 assists, a terrific ratio.

"I know that I play a lot of minutes. . . . It's definitely something I'm proud of," Bird said.

Handled with Care

Few can control a basketball as well as Bird. But dribbling is one of the most important (and basic) skills that all players must know. Teamwork is the key to a good and balanced offense. But there are many times when one player must be in control of the ball. Sometimes it is the point guard bringing the ball up the court. Other times it is another player taking on a defender one-on-one. Regardless, the ball handler needs to be able to move with the ball while also protecting it from defenders.

Becky Hammon (25) of the San Antonio Silver Stars takes on an Indiana Fever defender during a 2011 WNBA game.

Good ball handlers most often control the ball with their fingers rather than the palms of their hands. They can dribble with either hand and move quickly while also keeping their eyes up to see their teammates and opponents. They can dribble just as well to their right as their left. They can also pass with either hand and make a layup with either hand.

The Seattle Storm's Sue Bird brings the ball up the court against the Minnesota Lynx during the 2012 WNBA playoffs.

Quick Tip: Attack the Cone Zone

Good dribbling skills such as Sue Bird's can be improved through drills and practice. One popular drill involves setting up two lines of cones on the court, each cone 10 feet (3 m) from the next in a straight line. Find a partner and race each other through the cones by dribbling through them, first up and then back. Try to keep your head up while switching the ball from your right hand to your left hand. Always keep your body between the cone and the ball. This will improve speed and the ability to dribble with either hand.

By learning to use both hands well, a player can better protect the ball by keeping her body between the ball and an opponent.

Good ball handling skills prevent turnovers. They also allow a team to move the ball quickly around the court to find openings in a defense.

Time and again during her career, Bird has been able to dribble through multiple defenders, switch hands and directions, and then skillfully pass the ball to an open teammate or take an open shot. Ball handling skills are acquired through years of drills and practice. Those who have mastered those skills become some of the hardest players to stop.

"She can score, pass, and handle the ball, and she can lead," former Storm coach Lin Dunn said of Bird. "Her presence on the floor makes everyone better."

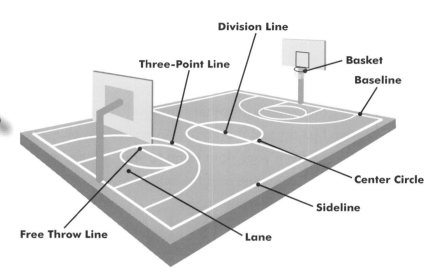

Division Line

Three-Point Line

Basket

Baseline

Center Circle

Sideline

Free Throw Line

Lane

baseline and sideline

These lines mark the borders of the court.

center circle

The tipoff takes place here. Only the two players taking the tipoff can be inside the circle.

division line

This line separates the court in half. Once the offense has possession in the opponent's side of the court, it must stay on that side.

free throw line

A player must stand behind this line, which is 15 feet from the backboard, while taking free throws.

lane

All players must be outside this area during a free throw. Offensive players can only be in the lane for three seconds at a time if not in possession of the ball.

three-point line

Shots made from beyond this arc are worth three points.

assist
A pass from one player to another that leads directly to a basket.

bank shot
A shot in which a player shoots the ball to make it bounce (bank) off the backboard into the basket.

defender
A player from the team without the ball trying to guard or stop a player from a team with the ball.

double-double
Recording double figures (10 or more) in two of these statistical categories: points, rebounds, assists, blocked shots, or steals.

draft
A system in which leagues spread incoming talent among every team.

layup
A shot in which a player lays the ball up into the basket or banks it off the backboard toward the hoop from a very short distance.

man-to-man defense
A defensive scheme in which defenders are assigned to guard a particular player from the other team when it has the ball.

rebound
To gain control of a missed shot.

scheme
A system of offense or defense, such as man-to-man defense.

steal
A play in which a defender takes the ball away from an opponent.

turnover
A mistake made by the team with the ball that costs that team possession of the ball.

zone defense
A defensive scheme in which defenders are assigned to guard an area (a zone) of the court rather than an individual opponent.

Glossary

Selected Bibliography

Allard, Marc. "Tina Charles shows rebounding flair." *Norwich Bulletin*. Gatehouse Media, Inc. 5 July 2012. Web. 27 Feb. 2013.

Jacobs, Jeff. "There's no stopping Maya Moore on the move." *Hartford Courant*. Hartford Courant. 29 Nov. 2010. Web. 27 Feb. 2013.

Scoggins, Chip. "What makes a good point guard?" *Star Tribune*. Star Tribune. 7 Feb 2012. Web. 27 Feb. 2013.

Further Readings

Goldberg, Jeff. *Bird at the Buzzer. UConn, Notre Dame and a Women's Basketball Classic.* Lincoln, NE: University of Nebraska Press, 2011.

Grundy, Pamela, and Susan Shackelford. *Shattering the Glass: The Remarkable History of Women's Basketball.* Chapel Hill, NC: University of North Carolina Press, 2007.

Oatman, R. S. *The Lindsay Whalen Story.* Cambridge, MN: Nodin Press, 2010.

Women's Basketball Coaches Association. *The Women's Basketball Drill Book.* Champaign, IL: Human Kinetics Publishers, 2007.

Web Links

To learn more about basketball, visit ABDO Publishing Company online at **www.abdopublishing.com**. Web sites about basketball are featured on our Book Links page. These links are routinely monitored and updated to provide the most current information available.

Places to Visit

Naismith Memorial Basketball Hall of Fame
1000 Hall of Fame Ave.
Springfield, MA 01105
(413) 781-6500
www.hoophall.com

Opened in 1968, this museum has exhibits about the sport's birth and development and has enshrined coaches and players from men's and women's college, professional, and international teams.

Women's Basketball Hall of Fame
700 Hall of Fame Drive
Knoxville, TN 37915
(865) 633-9000
www.wbhof.com

This facility was opened in 1999 and specifically honors the best players and coaches in the women's game. Nearly 150 women and men have been inducted.

Index

ABOUT THE AUTHOR

Doug Williams is a freelance writer based in San Diego, California. After graduating from Humboldt State University he worked as a newspaper reporter and editor for 33 years. He was honored by the San Diego Press Club for best sports story for a daily newspaper or Web site in 2012. This is his second book. He enjoys spending time with his wife, two adult daughters, and his golden retriever.